Legacies

Short Stories, Plays, and Prose

Gertrude R. Anderson

M.O.R.E. Publishers
St. Louis, Missouri

M.O.R.E. Publishers
P.O. Box 38285, St. Louis, MO 63138

Angelee Coleman Grider, Editor
Edwin Grider, Editor

ISBN 978-0-9830325-3-3

TABLE OF CONTENTS

Introduction   1

About the Author and Her Work   3

Legacy of Short Stories
Grandma Daisy   7

The Egg   12

Close To Her Bosom   18

A Spider In The Bath Tub   37

The Ride   39

Talk To The Trees   48

Legacy of Plays and Drama
The Road To Calvary   57

Fruits of the Spirit   69

Our Redeemer   75

The Thirteenth Disciple   79

Changed Mah (My) Name   87

LEGACIES
Introduction

People think of a legacy as being material gains that a family may leave to their offspring when one dies. I believe this is only a portion of the sum totals of one's inheritance.

It is good to be able to bestow material gains to one's offspring, and there is nothing wrong with that. But I also believe giving them a sense of who they are, and passing down certain events that the family has experienced and learned, will equally be an important legacy.

Families, telling stories about families, keep them together. When the stories are negative, prayerfully the family will learn from them. When the stories are positive, hopefully they will give someone something for which to strive. The most important thing one can give one's family, and friends, is a good true story. It is the only thing one can leave behind upon leaving this earth.

A legacy of unity and perseverance is greatly to be desired by most families, but whatever that legacy maybe, hopefully it will be one that will lift the human spirit. Hopefully it will inspire other family members to be the best they can.

About the Author and Her Work
Gertrude Richmond Anderson
Prologue

What more could be said about the author - Gertrude R. Anderson, other than she is a believer in the power of words? She interprets things well.

Anderson's love of reading, writing, and music was encouraged by her fifth grade teacher in the classrooms of the Chicago Public Schools.

Then just before World War II ended, she married Odie S. Anderson, now one of the Marshall County veterans of the Armed Forces. She and her husband lived on a farm and reared a family of eight.

Later, she returned to school and earned a degree in Elementary Education from Rust College in Holly Springs, Mississippi. She began a career teaching in the Head-Start Program, and eventually the Mississippi Public Schools.

She said that reading was her favorite hobby. "There is power in words," she said. "Words make a person *Think and Feel.*"

"I think about that God is the source of my strength and He is my protection. He leads me and guides me in the direction that He wants me to take."

After retiring from her career as a teacher, Anderson continued spending her time writing words. She wrote articles for the community. She also developed Biblical plays for her church's drama ministry where she wrote many poems, and praised God.

"The Road To Calvary" is one of the plays that she completed recently. It was presented first as a radio reading

3

and discussion piece on the Cayce Express Broadcast, 92.7 FM. That play and others were then placed within the publication of her book LEGACIES. The book includes elite choices of her short stories, plays, songs, prose and the inclusion of a local artist's work.

Projections: Enhancements of all literary work along with other authors' writings, rely upon promoting and appearances. A group of authors late in 2010, pooled ideas to promote positive literary outcomes of poetry readings, short play-lets, and book signings.

The segment, relevant to the community, was that artists' displays by the youths, adults and senior citizens were available for the birthday celebration of activist Ida B. Wells in support of the Ida B. Wells Museum. The event took place July 15, 2011 where the group was able to demonstrate their affiliation with the FW Coleman Theatre Club for senior adults.

Club members constantly helped Mrs. Anderson promote works and participation on the website – www.FWColemanTheatre.com. This was one of the highlights of her writing career since starting to work with professional directors and sponsors. Her church plays had formerly just been presented in the church with limited acting and just reading of lines. She finally saw her works reach maturity.

The **ROAD TO CALVARY** is one of the shorter plays, yet require the acting ability of more men than women. The local artist that collaborated with her was Terri Holt of Memphis, Tennessee.

Legacy of
Short Stories

Grandma Daisy

Stories are re-told by Gertrude Richmond Anderson

My name is Amy Williams. My family is only one of many African Americans who have lived here in "Sweet Water, Mississippi", with perhaps one difference. The Williams family lived on their same small farm for going on five generations.

Great Grandpa Williams bought this farm just after the civil war and the Williams family members have always lived here at one time or another.

Grandma Daisy, my Grandma Jennie's sister, and her daughter Flora lives in the old home house at this time. That old house has seen many repairs and fixing up down through the years, but it is still fairly comfortable. In the summer, the high ceilings keep the house cool and in the winter the house was hard to heat. Still it was home to most of us.

Grandma Daisy is the sole survivor of her generation. She is at the stage in her life where she tells everyone, "This may be my last time." This statement is often made when there is something to be done, and she wants to take a part in it. Or she says it when she wants to have her way, and say.

One day in the fall of 1992, Grandma Daisy, Flora (her daughter), and Grandma Daisy's granddaughter Wensie and I were sitting in the lounge of the local hospital waiting for Wensie's daughter Jean to deliver her first child. This was the beginning of the 6th generation of our family that we knew about. Jean's husband, Floyd, was in the army somewhere overseas. So he could not be there.

Jean said, "There are too much danger and diseases in the country where he is stationed for me to live there. Besides, I want to be with my family when the baby comes."

"The women in my family have a world of experience in family matters, and I want to have access to them all," she had told Floyd, in jest.

Amazingly though when Jean's labor pains started, her mother Wensie had driven her to the hospital in such a hurry, one would have thought she was going to put out a fire. Then when Grandma Daisy heard the news she wanted to go to the hospital to be with Flora. So Grandma Daisy followed in another car but not so fast.

"This may be the last time I'll see a new family member come into this world" she had said and insisted we bring her along. Of course, we didn't refuse to let her go. Remember, that just "might be her last time." Yes, she sure knew how to get her way.

While sitting there in the hospital lounge, I counted the multicolored tile blocks on the hospital floor several times, listened to the sounds of many footsteps echoing down the corridors, watched people hurrying to the six elevators and fidgeting in my seat. I then looked over to Grandma Daisy and smiled when I saw her dozing quietly with her mouth opened and her head lying on the big green sofa where we sat. She was oblivious to the traffic in the corridors.

Suddenly everything seemed to quiet down as my stomach started to rumble. "That's why people stopped walking in the hall," I thought to myself. "They have gone to lunch."

I touched Aunt Flora in her ribs and whispered, "I'm hungry. Let's go downstairs to the cafeteria and get something to eat."

"I'm a little hungry myself," she said. "I ate breakfast a long time ago." It was usual for most elderly people to get up early and eat early in the rural community.

"Let me wake up Mama," she said. She went to Grandma Daisy and shook her gently, so she would not be scared out of her wits.

"Wake up Mama. Let's go to lunch."

Grandma Daisy raised her head up, blinked her eyes several times and asked, "Is the baby here yet?"

"No," Aunt Flora told her. "We haven't heard a word from the doctor. They will let us know when it comes. Come on. We'll only be gone a little while. Maybe there will be some news when we get back."

We went to the elevator and walked inside of it. Aunt Flora pushed the first floor button that would carry us to where the cafeteria was located down stairs. I held on to a small railing on the side because elevators made me feel funny when they are going down. When we left the elevator, Aunt Flora and I walked with Grandma Daisy because she was past 90 years old and couldn't be hurried. Wensie rushed on ahead. I guess she didn't want to stand in the cafeteria line too long. After we ate lunch, we returned upstairs and continued to wait for a long time.

Fully awake and being satisfied with a tasty lunch under her belt, Grandma Daisy wanted to talk. She began by telling about other cousins and their children's births. Some of the names I knew; others I didn't. Grandma Daisy made sure we knew at least some of our kin.

Most of them had moved away, she said. "But I want you to know about them anyway. This will keep you from taking up with your kinfolks." That was her way of saying courting and marrying them.

Now, I was no spring chicken, but it seemed like the elder relatives could remember things that happened a long time ago better than they could some things that happened five minutes ago. That was true with Grandma Daisy. Since she was in a talking mood, we sat and waited until she had gathered her thoughts together.

"… So I can tell it just right," she said. Grandma Daisy was a long talker when she got started and sometimes told the same thing over and over again. Every now and then she would recall something we hadn't heard before. For instance, she told us she could remember when people worked a whole day for twenty-five (25) cents.

Grandma Daisy shifted her hips on the lounge sofa, got comfortable and collected her thoughts. "When I was a child, most of our family members met on my parents' farm on special days and Sunday evenings," she said.

"My daddy told us that he brought our mother there when they got married and she was only fifteen (15) years old. Now, in those days couples married young and they stayed together; not like today when one of them gets angry about anything, they are ready to get a divorce, she said.

"Honey, you have to have patience with people 'cause life is a learning lesson all the time," she said.

"We had large families then, and our children were our pride and joy. We never got bored because there was always something to do. We learned a lot of listening and doing. A lot of people now-a-days never learn anything because they don't listen, and do very little doing," she added.

"Well, on our special days at the farm, eventually someone would start telling stories about certain people in our family and had everyone laughing," she said.

"But there was a lesson to be learned in them, even though some of them were silly. Some of our family members called these stories 'glorified lies', but they did have an element of truth in them as I remember it," she qualified herself.

"Now there were a few rascals in our family, but there were also a lot of good honest people in it too."

She finally finished that series of introducing family members. The she began to tell another one. Either way, new or old, her stories always kept the family laughing, and also bound them together.

The Egg

Some people think that just because a person is reared in the country, they should know all there is to know about life on a farm. Right? Wrong! The assumption is not always so, especially with young children.

"My cousins, Carl and Tim," said Grandma Daisy, "were very devilish when they were teenagers and often took advantage of those who had not learned the facts surrounding living on the farm."

"Every now and then they would leave their farm and family, and go visit Uncle Charles and Aunt Susie on their farm. Uncle Charles and Aunt Susie had several older children and one young son named Cecil."

Now Cecil like many young children liked to tag along with the older children, especially Carl and Tim. Many times his presence would spoil their fun because Cecil told everything he saw or knew, especially about Carl and Tim.

Grandma Daisy's story continued. "One weekend the two boys came to visit their Uncle Charles and Aunt Susie. On this particular day, Cecil wanted to follow but the older boys said 'NO!' No matter what they said to Cecil though, when they looked around, he would still be following them everywhere they went. Finally, the boys gave in and told Cecil that he could stay with them for a 'little while'!'"

After the invitation and permission, Cecil ran to catch up with the older cousins. He was smiling all the way. Together the three boys went into the pasture and pestered the cows until the bull saw them. They barely made it through the fence, dragging Cecil with them before the bull reached the fence and began to paw on the ground with his feet where they stood and blew his nostrils at them. The boys however laughed and thought that was exciting!

Next they went to the pig pen and watched the sow and her piglets wallow in the mud. They climbed up on the fence and watched the mules and horses chase one another up and down the pasture.

On the way to the house, they saw an old gander and began to throw rocks at him. Then they ran when he chased them or tried to fly up in their faces.

Carl and Tim really wanted to go fishing, on this day, but they did not want Cecil to go with them. The last thing they wanted was for him to fall in the pond. As they approached the farm house, they boys decided to go by the hen house and collect any eggs they could find and carry them to Aunt Susie. Every nest had at least one egg in it, except the last one. Sitting on that nest was an old red hen. She would not let anyone near her.

"That hen is setting," said Tim. "See how she pecks at my hand when I try to look in her nest."

"Setting? What is that? What is that? What is that? What is that?" asked Cecil who was peeping around the door of the hen house.

"She is sitting on some eggs that will soon hatch into baby chicks, dummy," said Carl.

Cecil was fascinated by this knowledge because he had never given a thought to where chickens came from, at least not this way. He had seen the chicks pecking in the yard, scratching for bugs and worms, and bits of corn, but that was all that he knew.

"Can anybody sit on eggs and hatch some baby chicks?" he wanted know.

Carl winked his eye at Tim and answered with a straight face. "Of course they can, if anybody wanted some baby chicks bad enough."

"Come to dinner!" called Aunt Susie.

"Come on," said Tim. "I am hungry. Let's go eat!" They touched one another on the shoulder and raced for the kitchen, leaving Cecil stumbling behind.

After dinner, Carl and Tim's parents came to carry them home. The adventure with the eggs was almost forgotten, but not quite.

On the back porch of Uncle Charles and Aunt Susie's house stood an old sofa. It was used to relax on after a hard day's work in the fields. Being almost worn out, it had several sinks in it where the springs had fallen apart. Otherwise it was fairly comfortable for sitting.

Now Cecil had not forgotten the henhouse. After he

thought everyone was relaxing, he returned to the chicken house. He looked in the hen nests and found four new eggs. He gathered them carefully, put them in his cap and carried them to the sofa. He painstakingly put them in one sunken place in the sofa. He reasoned that four baby chicks would be all for which he could care. Very carefully he sat on the sofa, covering the hole in the sofa so he would not crush the eggs. Then he waited for his eggs to hatch into baby chicks.

Aunt Susie, his mother, came to the door and saw him sitting there. She did not say anything to him at first. She was glad that he was not underfoot and in her way while she cooked the food for dinner. When dinner was ready, she called everyone to the dinner table.

Cecil answered her and said, "I'm not hungry!" That was unusual for Cecil because he was a big eater.

"When you get hungry, it will be on the stove," Aunt Susie said. She continued to do her chores in the house.

Later though that evening, Aunt Susie went on the porch again and was surprised to see Cecil still sitting in the same place on the old sofa.
"Why are you sitting in the same place on that old sofa?" she asked.

"Nothing," answered Cecil. "I just like to sit here."

"Well you had better come and eat your food before someone else eats it," she said. She went back into the house.

Darkness came. Again Aunt Susie came on the porch and Cecil was still sitting in the very same place on the old sofa. She knew then that something was going on with Cecil and that sofa. He had never sat in one place for over ten minutes in his life.

"Alright young man," she demanded, "what is going on with you?" She walked near him. "Cecil, get up and come into the house." Cecil kept sitting there.

"You heard me. Come into the house!"

Cecil kept his seat and started to cry.

"Now what are you crying about?" she asked.
"I can't get up," he replied. "I have to keep sitting on my eggs!"

"What are you talking about?" shouted Aunt Susie.

With tears still running down his cheeks, he sobbed, "Carl and Tim said that if I sat on some eggs long enough, I could hatch some baby chicks just like the red hen in the henhouse. I want some baby chicks of my own to play with."

Uncle Charles had heard the commotion on the porch. As he came outside, he wondered why Susie looked enraged. Aunt Susie made Cecil get up. Uncle Charles saw the eggs and started to laugh, especially when he heard Cecil say he could not get up. Uncle Charles pointed to the eggs and laughed harder at the sight.

"Who ever heard of a boy sitting on eggs to hatch baby chicks?" he laughed.

Aunt Susie grabbed Cecil by the arm and demanded, "Get your behind in the house. You can't hatch eggs like a hen. Those boys need a switch put on their behinds for fooling a young boy like Cecil.

Uncle Charles still laughed even harder as Aunt Susie

pulled the shamed-face Cecil's arm into the house. "Go wash your face, eat your supper, and then carry your silly behind to bed!"

The next time Carl and Tim came for a visit, Aunt Susie "lit into them like a buzz saw" for teasing young Cecil. They tried to keep from laughing when she told them what Cecil had done, but the laughter was too hard to keep inside. Cecil was ashamed and angry at himself for letting his cousins play that trick on him. Yet, he stopped following them for a little while!

Even now, as grown men, when the cousins get together, they still get a chuckle out of the story of Cecil and the eggs. Cecil is even now able to laugh with them about the memory. Cecil said that the lesson he learned was not to go where you are not wanted, especially with older boys.

Close To Her Bosom
By
Gertrude R. Anderson

Psalms 37:3
Trust in the Lord and do good; so shalt thou dwell in this land and verily thou shalt be free."

This was the story of two families, and how they overcame obstacles in their lives. It was one of Grandma Daisy's favorite stories.

The constant patter of falling rain aroused Etta from her sleep. She rose from her bed, put on her robe and went through the door of her bedroom, then out of the back door to the porch. The sweet smell of the falling rain drenching the dry earth brought the sensation of life being reborn in the dust that lay beneath.

She leaned her head back and inhaled deeply of the dirt fragrance. It had been a hot, dusty week, so the rain was more than welcome.

Pulling her robe tighter around her chubby, brown body, Etta went to the swing that was attached to the ceiling of the porch, and sat down. A soothing wind was coming from the west, bringing with it the coolness she sought as she reflected on her life. She looked across the way to her neighbor, Samantha Stewart's window. She could see Samantha moving around in her kitchen. Etta could also smell the rich aroma of coffee boiling, and tasty rolls baking in her neighbor's oven.

Samantha was a quiet, tall, brown-skinned woman, and also Etta's best friend. They grew up together as children, went to school, and married in the same year. Samantha gave birth to a son two years after her marriage and named him "Ross". Six months later, Etta gave birth to a son and named him "Robert". They all lived in the same community and on the same farm. This was common in their younger days.

Etta's husband, James Walton, was still in bed asleep. Since he retired from the railroad, he enjoyed sleeping late whenever he could. During his years on the railroad, he was always in a rush getting to work on time. He didn't have to do that anymore, and couldn't if he wanted to do so. He now worked at home at his own pace.

While sitting in the swing, Etta recalled some special events in their lives. She pushed the swing back and forth and spoke of the time when she and Samantha had married. They were both young and thought they were marrying the men of their dreams. They were sure they would be happy forever. There was only one thing that bothered Etta.

James was not interested in buying a home, even though she was. The young couple had begun their marriage living as tenant farmers, but she did not want to spend their entire life living like that. Already Samantha and Ed were making plans to get their own place.

The young women had married fresh from their parents' homes and had been taught that the husband would be the head of the home. They were also taught that it was their duty as wives to follow each husband's lead.

The young men had been taught, by several of the older men that the wife's place was in the kitchen. Several of the "no-count men" had given their advice and even added something extra - "To keep control of your woman, keep her barefoot and pregnant." Of course the women did not have privy to that advice.

Being a ruler of his home was not a big deal with Ed. He and Samantha began together to make plans to get their own farm. "Two heads are better than one," he said to his friends when they gave him their advice.

When James heard what Ed and Samantha were undertaking, James felt it would be too much of a sacrifice to do the same. James had seriously taken his "man-training" from old buddies, and did not bother to discuss home ownership with Etta. When Etta brought up the subject, James replied, "Some day, but not in the near future."

When Etta brought up the subject again of ownership, he immediately began to point out, one by one, the hardship they would have to endure, and spoke of every negative consequence of which he could think, trying to convince Etta that it was not a good idea at the time. But Etta could always think of something that would be worse if they did not try. Her comments would often upset James and he would storm out of the house and stay away for hours.

Many times Etta and Samantha would sit at one or the other's kitchen table and talk on Sunday evenings after church services. They each agreed that "It helps to have someone to talk to who understands how you feel." Together they would bear one another's burdens and pray together. They also enjoyed discussing the laughter and the gossip in the neighborhood.

After a few years of saving, Ed and Samantha moved on their own, small farm with their son, Ross Lee. Immediately Ed began to shape his farm the way he wanted, and Samantha did likewise with the small house that came with it.

When Etta and Samantha met again, Etta said, "I don't mean to criticize my husband, but it seems the only things of importance to James are trucks, cars, fancy clothes, and a night out with his cronies. I wish I could say or do something that would make him see things as I see them.

There is a reason why I continue to pester James about owning our own home in this community. I have noticed that when the people who did not have a place of their own, become too feeble to work the fields as tenants, they were told to move elsewhere, and younger people were given the house and the field.

If they had no place to go, they were sent to a place called 'the poor house'. There they had to depend on the generosity of the community to supply their needs. Sometimes their needs were met, but many times they were not."

One day Samantha and Etta rode by the place where the elderly poor were kept. They saw the poor wretches sitting on the sagging porch of a dilapidated building, covered with raggedy blankets and dirty quilts. The sight of those old, used-up people sitting there made them feel so sad that they could not go by there again unless they had something to share with them. The two women did not have clothing to share but did carry farm produce at least once a week.

Etta said to Samantha, "My Lord, I certainly don't want to end up in a place like that!"

After visiting and observing the condition of those

homeless, old people, Etta pleaded with Ed to please talk some sense into James or they would surely end up in the same predicament. Ed though would not touch that subject with a "ten-foot pole". He felt that it would damage his and Ed's friendship if he sided with Etta.

Once, Ed did tell James about his and Etta's differences of opinion. In frustration, James said, "Women don't know anything about business. Their place is in the kitchen and seeing about a family. I'm head of my house and I'll operate things as I see fit! That woman is driving me crazy with her nagging!" Ed quietly changed the subject.

As time passed, Etta started to get discouraged and gave up on her dreams of owning her home, but Samantha would not let her. Samantha encouraged her by saying, "It will happen. One day you will get your own place. Maybe the time is not right yet."

"When will it happen?" asked Etta. "It seems to me that it will never happen."

"I don't know, but it will. I can feel it. Don't give up," said Samantha. "I have got to go now. See you in church."

The years passed and the couples grew older. So did the sons of each couple. In fact, one morning Samantha knocked on Etta's door wearing the biggest grin Etta had ever seen. "Girl you are lit up like a Christmas tree. What's going on?" asked Etta.

"My baby Ross Lee is getting married. I don't know whether to laugh or to cry."

"Do I know her? Is she a nice girl…I mean who is the girl? Those boys can't keep to themselves who their last dates were," laughed Etta.

"It's Betty. You know that little girl who sings so nicely in the church choir," said Samantha.

"Betty Rolland! Yes, I know her. Ross Lee is crazy about her! He made a good choice. Well, I declare, time sure passes fast. Little Ross Lee is getting married."

"I want you to help me get everything ready, 'cause I want my son to have a beautiful wedding. Betty's mother and I are getting together tomorrow, and I want you to come with us," said Samantha.

"I would have been mad as a bear if you had left me out of this," said Etta.

"Well, I have to hurry. See you tomorrow!"

Ross Lee and Betty were married on Thanksgiving Day. The young couple moved in with Samantha and Ed. A year later, Samantha and Ed made another change in their life. Ed came home with a big grin on his face.

"You look like the cat that swallowed the canary. What is going on?" Samantha asked.

"I have a new job. That's what's going on," he replied.

"You already have a job, here on the farm," said Samantha.

"I know," he said. "I am going to start work on the railroad. But listen, with a new job we will soon be able to finish paying for this little farm."

"Ross Lee, with you and a little help from me, everything will work just fine. Ross Lee is already plowing the fields almost as good as I do. I can tell him what to do on my days off. Everything will work out fine, just wait and see!"

"Are you sure you can do this?" asked Samantha.

"Sure we can," laughed Ed. "Just wait and see."

The following year when the farming season began, Ross Lee and Betty took charge of the crops while Ed worked on the railroad, and Samantha took a job as the cook at the nursing home in the town of Lewisville.

When the farm was paid for, Ross Lee and Betty rented a house in Lewisville. They decided to rent out the farm to another young family.

Soon, Etta and James's son, Robert, also got it in his head that he was also grown enough to take care of himself, and of course take care of a wife. James was happy that Robert had matured enough to at least want to settle down. He was also glad that Robert had stopped chasing every girl in the county. But unlike Ed, James did not want a young couple living with him and Etta under the same roof. James began to make other plans.

Before farming season began again, James made a trip to Lewisville, the small town not far from where they lived. He was looking for a small house that was for rent. He contacted the owner and made the necessary arrangements to rent it. He didn't tell Etta because he did not want to hear her discuss what she wanted again.

His only thought was, "Don't let that young couple move in with Etta and me."

Robert had told his father, James, that the girl's name was Lettie Jean, and that he intended to marry her. When James told Etta, she said with surprise, "Married? Did you say Married? He told you that?"

"Yes, he did," said James. "We had a man to man talk last

week."

"Wait until I tell Samantha about this," said Etta. "We gonna put the show on the road again! Is he going to marry Mildred?"

"No!" he said. "The girl's name is Lettie Jean."

"I'll be back in an hour," said Etta as she rushed out of the door and started to Samantha's house. Etta could not wait to tell Samantha that Robert and Lettie Jean were moving close to them.

Samantha was shocked when she heard the news. "What farm was near Lewisville?" she wanted to know.

"That is not so far," said Etta. "Well, I will see you later!"

"Why can't James think like Ed?" she thought to herself. James is a good husband in many ways, but he can't seem to grasp what is important and what is not. Of course she couldn't say that to Samantha. That would make her disloyal to James.

Robert and Lettie Jean were married at Calvary Baptist Church. The following week they moved in the house near Lewisville and set up housekeeping. Etta lived with them sometimes on weekends. Soon after they had settled in, Lettie Jean found a job working in a restaurant. There she learned to make the fancy dishes that were served there. Her specialty was dinner rolls because the smell of the rolls baking in the ovens drew customers almost immediately at lunch time. It wasn't long before the restaurant had as many customers as they could handle.

Back on the farm, Etta was feeling down in the dumps. She took down her fishing pole and went to the pond to fish for a while. But today, she got no joy from her favorite past time. She left the pond, stopped at her mailbox, and pulled out the mail. Buried among the sale papers was a letter from her Aunt Margaret who lived in Memphis, Tennessee.

This was unusual, for Aunt Margaret seldom wrote to anyone. Etta opened the letter and read it. Aunt Margaret was letting her know that her Uncle Austin on her father's side of the family had died and the funeral was scheduled to take place in two days at Christian Baptist Church in Lewisville, the church where Ross Lee and Betty attended.

Etta told James about her uncle's death and made plans to attend the funeral. James had to work and he could not attend, so Etta went alone. After the funeral service, Aunt Margaret invited the relatives to visit with her in Memphis. They needed to meet those who lived a long distance from the family. Etta went with them.

She later told Samantha, "Child that was a real experience. Some of my relatives acted real citified and important, and some were real friendly. There were some who were right out nutty, but fun to be around. I left and promised them I would keep in touch."

One night while James was out with his friends, Etta became bored and took out the family album. As she looked at the pictures, she thought of Aunt Margaret. The next day Etta planned to visit her in Memphis. She had not seen her since Uncle Austin's funeral. When Etta arrived, Aunt Margaret was glad to see her and asked her to spend the night.

She said, "Not this time, but I will come back another time."

They sat and talked a long time, at least Aunt Margaret did. In her conversation, she mentioned Lewisville. Etta, whose thoughts had begun to wander, came back to the present moment when Aunt Margaret mentioned Lewisville.

"Austin and I have property there," she said, "but it needs a lot of work done on it. I don't have the money now to keep up the taxes, so I am thinking about selling it."

When she said that, an idea flashed in Etta's mind. She asked timidly, "Would you sell it to me, Aunt Margaret? I can't pay you all at one time, but I can pay you month by month."

"Well, yes, Etta," she said. "Might as well sell it to you as anybody else."

Excited, Etta said, "I'll be back next weekend Aunt Margaret, and finalize the deal. As of now, consider the property sold." She left Aunt Margaret's house and kept her plans, "close to her bosom."

On her way home, Etta stopped at Lewisville and went to the nursing home there. She applied for a job, and was hired to work on the night shift. The next morning, at the breakfast table, Etta casually told James that she had taken a job at the nursing home in Lewisville, during the night shift. She waited for his comments.

James sat and thought for a few minutes, then said, "On one condition. You still have to work in the fields and I want some food cooked before you leave."

Etta agreed to his conditions. She had expected him to be angry and was relieved when he did not make any objections.

That night, she began her first night on the new job. She was already tired, but the night shift was quiet. The majority of the patients slept through the night. Her tiredness soon disappeared when she thought of her mission. It seemed an unseen force was pushing her forward.

That weekend, Etta went back to Aunt Margaret's house in Memphis and made her first payment on the property. Aunt Margaret gave her the deed to two acres of land in Lewisville. On her way home she stopped at Ross Lee and Betty's house. She asked them to listen to something important that she had to say.

"First of all," she said, "What I am about to say will have to stay within these walls. Nobody is to know about this."

"Not even Uncle James?" asked Ross Lee.

"Especially him," said Etta. With that said, Etta proceeded to tell them what she had done. She asked for their cooperation. "The lot next door now belongs to me. Garbage and all!"

Six months later, a man with a bulldozer came to the lot on Elm Street and cleaned away everything on it. Samantha stood at Ross Lee's backdoor and watched. When Ed saw it later, he said, "I wonder what are the people who own that lot gonna do with it?"

When James' son Robert came to visit Ross Lee, he asked the same question.

"I don't know," said Ed, "but I'm glad to see it cleaned up. I know Ross Lee is glad."

Almost a year went by before there was activity again on the lot. Then one day Samantha saw Ross Lee and two other men unloading lumber and stacking it in piles on the lot. She waved to Ross Lee and yelled, "How is Betty doing?

"Just fine," he called back, and continued to stack the lumber. Afterwards, they left.

When Samantha saw Etta at church the following Sunday she mentioned that she saw Ross Lee and two other men stacking lumber on the lot next door to Ross Lee's.

Samantha said, "That boy of mine works hard. The company he works for is real busy these days, and how is your family, Etta?"

"Just fine. As for James and me, James stays gone a lot on the railroad where he began to work with Ed, but everyone is doing good. Thank God!"

"Did you know they were working together?" asked Samantha.

"Yes," Etta said but could hardly keep a straight face while talking to her best friend. She had to keep her secret, "close to her bosom."

Six months later, while at Ross Lee and Betty's home, Samantha was awakened by the sound of hammers. She looked next door and saw a woman and two men starting a foundation for a house. She could not see who the woman was. Before the week was out, they had the sides and part of the roof on it. Samantha's curiosity was killing her. No one she had talked to knew whose house was being built.

Etta continued to make the payments to Aunt Margaret, and gave Ross Lee whatever she had left of her salary so he could buy materials for the house. As an employee for the lumber company, he could get material at a discount.

James didn't ask Etta about her salary. He didn't want her to ask about the money he made on his job, or how he was spending it. He told her once when she asked, "I am paying the bills, and giving you money to spend as you like and keep a good garden. Everything is doing fine. Aren't you satisfied?" With this said, they kept the peace.

Every evening when Samantha came to Ross Lee and Betty's home from her job, she sat on her back porch swing and watched the men work on the house next door. At last the house was finished. The next day a man came with a small tractor, plowed the acre out back of the new house and made rows for planting.

Two months later, Etta woke up early and went into the kitchen to make breakfast. James was still asleep. She made a tasty breakfast of ham with red-eye gravy, grits, eggs, grape jelly, biscuits, and steaming hot coffee. The aroma brought James to the table in a hurry.

"James," Etta began, "I want to talk a little business with you when I get back from work." She hurried out the door. She didn't want to be late at the job.

James was curious at her request. He thought she had found out he had been playing a few games of "Funny Cards" with his cronies and had lost a few dollars. Later he sighed a sigh of relief when she didn't mention "Money".

The next morning, Etta began by saying, "James we have been married for over 20 years and I have been wanting a home of my own all that time."

"Let's not get into that again," snapped James.

"Well, I know how you feel," said Etta, and I am not asking you again, to do something you don't want to do, but tomorrow I am moving into my new house. You are welcome to come with me. If not, I am sorrow. I love you and I hope you will come with me."

30

She got up from the table, got her coat, and got ready to leave. James was dumbfounded.

"Hey! Wait a minute. Not so fast. You have got a lot of explaining too do about that statement you just made. A house? How did you get a house? And where is it? This conversation ain't nothing like over!"

"I will tell you all about it when I get home," Etta called over her shoulder. "I am almost late for work. I am working day shift for this month."

After work, Etta did not go straight home. She went by Ross Lee and Betty's house. Samantha was visiting them when she knocked on the door. When Samantha came to the door, she said, "Come on in."

"No!" Etta said. "I want you to go home with me for a change."

Samantha laughed, "I can't go out into the country today child. I am dead tired."

Etta smiled and said, "You won't have far to go. Just step next door!"

"Etta, you are joking. You mean to tell me that cute little new house next door is yours?"

"Yes, it is. After all these years, do you think I would joke about something like that? Here is my key. Let's go inside."

The two friends went inside and looked in every room of the house, then sat down. Samantha cried when Etta told her story about how she finally got her house.
Samantha asked, "Why did you keep it such a secret? I am your closet friend."

"I know," said Etta, "but I couldn't tell you until I was sure everything was gonna be alright. It seems every time I tell my plans, something or someone would do something to mess it up. Not that you would, but I couldn't tell you and not tell James. I had to keep it close to my bosom."

"You haven't told James?" whispered Samantha?

"No. You know how he is. I couldn't take any chances that anything would spoil what I was working on. I told him this morning that I was moving into my house tomorrow."

"Tomorrow? Girl I will get to cooking right away so your helpers will have some food to eat when they are finished moving your stuff. Girl, you have made my day. Just wait until Ed hears about this. He will be as happy as a jay bird when he hears you and James will be living next door, to Ross Lee and Betty."

Etta left. She had an explanation to make to James. But it would be sometimes before she could do it. James did not come home as usual. That night, a rail coupling crushed one of his legs while he was on the job and he had to be carried to the hospital. Etta sat by his side as the doctors tried to save his leg.

Although James was outdone by Etta's secret, when he left the hospital, he moved into the house on Elm Street with Etta. She seldom left his side. Ed, on his off days, was James' constant companion when Etta had to be away. Together they made plans for planting a large vegetable garden next door.

The doctor couldn't save James's leg. They had him fitted for an artificial leg as soon as his stump healed. That ended his career as a railroad employee. He was put on disability and tried to adjust to life with one leg. That was not easy. At times the stump would get uncomfortable or irritated, and he had to take the artificial leg off. After a while, he began to leave it off all together, and walk on crutches.

Soon James, and Ed on his off days, began to work in the garden. They planted everything they could think of that would grow there. Everyday they would meet there and plan their day. Together they grew vegetables and supplied the entire neighborhood with fresh produce from their garden.

Three years after the move to Elm Street, Ed suffered a heart attack. One week later, he had another attack and died. Samantha grieved for Ed a long time. She loved him very much. James and Etta stood by her and helped where they could. Samantha continued to cook at the nursing home. As time passed, James' leg was getting better, but he truly missed his friend Ed. Ed's death had made him depressed, and that worried Etta.

While sitting at the breakfast table one morning, Etta discussed the problem with Samantha at length and tried to think of ways to pull James out of his depression. Suddenly Etta had an idea. Overcome with excitement, she said to Samantha, "Sam, let's start our own business so we both can be at home."

"James looks so lonesome and sad since Ed passed. He is not as spry and interested in the garden anymore as he used to be. I worry about him when I am at work. This situation is getting me down in spirit."

Samantha replied, "Girl I need a change. I really do since Ross Lee has moved to Ohio."

"We can use your house for the business," Etta suggested.

"A business?" asked Samantha. "What can we do at home? We don't have any skills."

"Of course we do," said Etta. "We are two of the best darn cooks in this county. The 1980's have grown something that we haven't had before, women who don't cook or can't and working wives that don't have the time to cook a decent meal, if they knew how."

With that said, both women started to laugh. "You know that is true. We can do this. I know we can," said Etta. "Everybody have a fit over your rolls. Samantha, just think, rolls selling over one dollar a dozen and my cakes. Everybody says they are the best cakes that they ever tasted."

The more Etta talked, the more Samantha could see their own business come into view. "We will have all the business we can handle from our own church members. Someone is always asking us to cook something when there is an activity at the church that calls for food. I think it will work," said Samantha.

"Let's give it a try. If you can succeed with that wild scheme of yours in secret, we can succeed with this one in public. Alright, I'll work with you. Let's at least give it a try."

Samantha became convinced and said, "Girl you are something!" The two women sat like two little children and discussed their plans.

The following Sunday, Etta announced in church that she and Samantha were starting a business. She said that they would be available to cook anyone's favorite meal, "just put in the order and when you want to pick it up." The business would be called Samantha and Etta's Dinners To Order.

When the business opened, Etta kept the books and

Samantha was the treasurer. Both women did the cooking. When they mentioned their plan to James, he liked the idea. He contacted several of his friends who were retirees as himself, to help in the vegetable garden.

They helped to keep the weeds out and pick the vegetables to use in the cooking business. Etta and Samantha kept the ovens going with the rolls, pies, and cakes. They kept the pots boiling with the fresh vegetables from the garden.

"That had been five years ago," Etta thought. "Time sure flies." Then Etta's mind came back to the present. She got up from the swing on the porch and went inside to prepare breakfast and wake up James. Since that time and the success of their business, they had secured a license, bought a larger oven and added two rooms to Samantha's house for their cooking area. They also hired four women to work as cooks, and helpers under the supervision of Samantha. The business was good!

After eating breakfast one morning, Etta dressed and went back to the swing. The smell of Samantha's coffee continued to plague her. "Oh well," she thought, "I have time for a cup of coffee with Samantha." She tipped-toed through the wet grass to Samantha's kitchen door.
"Good morning, girlfriend," she called.

"Come on in," answered Samantha. Etta opened the door and went inside. Samantha brought two cups and poured coffee into each one. "This is going too be a long day," said Etta, as she took a sip.

"Those basketball players are gonna be mighty hungry after the game tonight. I bet there will be a big crowd because Michael Jordan is gonna be playing."

"No joking?" said Samantha.

"No joking," responded Etta.

They looked out of the window and saw the four cook helpers coming to work. Etta sat her coffee cup down.

"Come on girlfriend; let's get this show on the road. We have a contract to feed those players. Now keep that close to your bosom."

"Etta are you joking?" asked Samantha.

"Honey, do you think I would joke about something like that? Remember, I keep the books. Girl we just might be on TV," said Etta. They both laughed and hurried to the kitchen to begin their day.

A Spider in the Bath Tub
"A Story for Children"

Jimmy went into the bathroom to take a bath. He saw something trying to climb onto the smooth surface of the tub. It was a spider. Every time the spider went up on the side of the tub just a little, it slid back down to the bottom.

Looking closely, Jimmy saw that the spider had what looked like a big head supported by eight hairy, long legs.

From where did the spider come? Why was it there? Were there others in the bathroom? Jimmy wanted to know. He looked on the floor. He looked in the waste basket. He looked under the sink, and on the towel rack.

He had heard that spiders like to hide in dark places. He opened the door of the bathroom and looked around in the place where the wood came together around the door frame. He saw no spiders.

Jimmy decided to get his book about spiders from the bookshelf. He read that there were many different kinds of spiders. They had strange names such as crab spiders, fisher spiders, jumping spiders, and wolf spiders.

He read that when a male jumping spider wanted to attract a female spider, he would raise his abdomen like a balloon and sways from side to side. Each female spider spins a different kind of egg sac. In the sac, young spiders hatched. They would come out of the sac.

The young spiders would immediately begin spinning lines to get where they wanted to go. However this special spider thought that he could go anywhere. He probably wondered in a place from which he could not get out.

Jimmy picked the spider up with a paper towel. Then

Jimmy threw it outside into the grass. Jimmy hoped that the spider would find some friends there.

The Ride

Note: This is not presented as a certain style of philosophy. It is literature passed from one generation to another. Grand Mama Daisy remembers other family stories also. This one is retold by Wensie, her sister Jenny's granddaughter.

I guess everyone in my generation remember December 7, 1941. That was the bombing of Pearl Harbor in Hawaii. What followed was World War II. It affected everyone in the United States.

Those on the farm where I lived began to grow larger crops, and worked longer hours in the fields to support the war effort. Being a teenager, the extra work did not bother me as much as it did the older people in the fields, but in one situation, the effects of the war did.

At our school that particular year we had the winning basketball team in the county. Before the year 1942 was over, all of our boys on the basketball team had been inducted into the armed forces except two players.

One of them had a heart condition. We never knew why the other player was "turned down". That was the term that was used for the men who did not pass the examination. As soon as a young man turned 18 years old they were drafted into service in the Army, Navy, or the Air Force.

It was a lonely school year for the girls and it continued to be for a long time. The majority of our male cousins were inducted also... The older girls began to move into the house of the older relatives, and they went to search for jobs. Though the war was an important element, this story is about my seventeen year old cousin, Nick.

After Grandpapa Walter passed away, Nick went to live with Grandma Jenny. Those two got along just like two peas in a pod. As a result of their friendship, Grandma Jenny promised Nick when he turned 18 years old; she would give him Grandpapa's old car that stood in the front yard, just where he left it.

"But" she said, "You will also have to be 18 years old before you can get your driver's license."

Needless to say, Nick waited patiently for his birthday to come. Grandma Jenny told him she had been waiting for someone to drive her where she wanted to go, in Grandpapa Walter's old car. She also was waiting for someone to learn to beat her father's small drum that he called his "healing drum". His Cherokee father had taught him to use it when someone was sick.

The wait didn't bother her too much about not using the car because Grandpapa Walter's memory was too strong in her mind. He loved that old car! He was always tinkering with it. Furthermore, Grandma Jenny could not drive.

When one of the other male cousins asked her "Why did you promise to give Nick the car?" She answered, "Nick is willing to help me here on the farm and does not get an attitude or sass me when I ask him to do some of the work."

That ended the conversation, for the boys spent their time playing baseball or racing the horses across the pasture when they finished their chores.

Grandpapa Walters' old car needed some repairs. The upholstery had begun to rot from sitting in the sun of summer and the cold of winter. Since he died, no one had attempted to repair it, mainly because Grandma Jenny would not let anyone touch it.

The time came when she changed her mind and asked the local mechanic to come visit her, take a look at the car, and tell her if he could fix it. If he could, she wanted him to take it to his shop and fix it. So it could run again.

She also wanted him to put new upholstery on the seats and outfit it with a set of new tires. With the war on, she didn't know if the mechanic could get the tires, but she was sure he had some from another used car. She wanted it to look nice when she passed her neighbor's house or rode in it when she went to a church gathering.

One day the mechanic came and pulled the car with his old wrecking truck. Then about a month later, the mechanic brought it home. It ran like an oiled sewing machine. The mechanic had painted it a bright shinning black color and fitted the seats with a pretty blue fabric.

When we heard that Grandma Jenny's car was back at her house, we children couldn't wait to see it. Believe me, it was a sight to see!

The car sat like a landmark in Grandma's front yard. Cousin Nick reminded all of us that the car was going to be his as soon as he turned 18 and got his driving license. He also reminded us that he would be the one driving Grandma where she wanted to go. There was another reason cousin Nick was anxious to get behind the wheel of the car. He wanted to impress a certain girl in our community.

While he waited for his birthday to come, he rubbed and polished that car every day until we thought he was going to rub all of that new paint off of it.

It was almost six months later before Grandma Jenny let him do a practice drive on the back road of our community. She told him he needed the practice before he applied for his driving license. Cousin Nick drove alone those bumpy roads thinking and day-dreaming of the serious courting he was planning on doing.

Finally his birthday came, but also on that day he received a letter from the United States War Department ordering him to report to a service camp for a physical examination. The letter also said that if he passed the physical, he would be inducted immediately into the Army. Cousin Nick was disappointed. He hadn't expected to be called so soon. He knew things were not going too well for the United States at that time because everywhere one could look; there was a sign that said, "Uncle Same Needs You." Cousin Nick was scheduled to report to the camp on the following week. However, the day after his birthday, he also went to apply for his driver's license. He took the test, passed it, and went home with the license in his pocket.

The following Sunday, he made plans to visit the special girl that he had been thinking about. The Saturday before he finished his chores, he also went to work on some of the things he had been putting off. He wanted things to be in order before he left for duty in the Army. He knew Grandma Jenny would let things remain as they were until he could come home again.

The next day was Sunday and Cousin Nick came out of his room early. He ate breakfast, did his morning chores, and went to the car to give it another good polishing.

Later in the day, he began to get dressed for his date. He left his room smelling like a perfume factory. His shoes were shining like glass and his pants and shirt were starched and ironed.

When Grandma Jenny saw him, she gave him a compliment. Then she proceeded to give him her "Do's and Don'ts" concerning the car.

Cousin Nick smiled like a cat when a cat sees a mouse. When she gave him the keys to the car and pronounced it "His", he went to it, cranked it up, and began to drive it down the road that led to the special girl's house.

We younger teens watched him drive away, wishing we could have gone with him to ride in the car also. We wanted our friends to see us, and to wave to them as we rode by with our arms hanging out of the window.

But Cousin Nicks' day did not go as he had planned. It seems that he forgot to tell the girl he was coming for a visit. When he arrived at her door, all laid back and dressed up, another young man was sitting in the girl's sitting room. The girl invited him to come inside, and that was as far as the conversation went. The girl did not ask Cousin Nick to stay, nor did she ask the other young man to leave. They just sat and looked at one another. Finally Cousin Nick decided to leave. He drove off disappointed. He hadn't even gotten a chance to have a conversation with the girl. When we heard about it later, we laughed and said, "He learned a lesson that day - not to go to a girl's house when one is not invited."

Cousin Nick drove around the neighborhood and picked up his friends, Jerry and Hubert. They went to a ball game. After that, he came home. Time seemed to go quickly. Soon there was only two days before Cousin Nick was scheduled to leave for his army physical. He picked up Jerry and Hubert, began to ride around the community, and began to say good-bye to his neighbors. He told them to "keep an eye out for Grandma Jenny" while he was away.

During the first part of the war years, if there was only one male in the home, the army was reluctant to take that one male away. Grandma Jenny had made arrangements though for one of our older cousins and his wife to move in with her if Cousin Nick had to stay in the army.

The day of his departure came. The bus that carried the young men to be examined was scheduled to leave late in the afternoon. So Cousin Nick thought he had time go "goof off" until that time came. He picked up his buddies Jerry and Hubert. They decided to ride around in the neighborhood for the last time before the bus came.

"How fast will this car go?" Jerry wanted to know.

Of course Cousin Nick did not know. He had only driven it on the rugged country roads. "I don't know but let's find out."

The thoughts of Grandma Jenny's "Do's" and "Don'ts" flew out of Cousin Nick's mind. He turned the car around and headed for the smooth surface of the State Highway. Other young men that we knew had done some stupid things when they received their Army induction notice. I guess Cousin Nick decided to have his last fling also. As he drove on the bumpy surface of the dirt road, Jerry played his harmonica and Hubert sang.

When they passed someone they knew, Hubert hung his arm out of the window, waved and shouted silly words at them. Finally the friends reached the smooth surface of the highway, and drove the car onto it.

"Put your foot to the pedal," shouted Jerry.

"Let her roll," urged Hubert.

Cousin Nick got caught up in the moment and did what his friends encouraged him to do. One witness said later, "Those boys and that shiny black car passed us like a bat out of torment."

Cousin Nick raced that car, passing everyone on the highway. Luckily, other motorists got out of the way when they saw the car coming their way. The young men were having so much fun racing, they didn't notice a policeman heading their way. When they did, they tried to slow down, but went off the smooth surface. They hit the loose gravel beside it and lost control of the car.

The car turned over and over until it finally stopped when it hit the side of a dirt bank. Miraculously, all three young men climbed out of the car, dusty as rats in a flour barrel. They did not have a scratch on them. Cousin Nicks last fling almost got him killed! The car was now a twisted piece of metal, bolts and broken glass.

They couldn't believe their eyes, when they came to their senses, and looked at it.

"God just was not ready for us," said Cousin Nick, "but I know Grandma Jenny will be ready for me; and it's not going to be pretty."
When the family received the news about the wreck, Grandma Jenny almost fainted. The first thing she wanted to know was "Did anyone get hurt?"

When she found out that the boys were alright, she began to shout, "Thank the Lord!" Then she began to fuss the rest of the day. No one could shut her up. She repeated over and over, "That boy tore up that car the minute I told him it was his, and had only driven it one day without me telling him how to handle it. Then he almost got his fool self killed!"

When Cousin Nick came home that evening, he could not hold his head up. He knew Grandma Jenny was truly hurt. He had destroyed her beloved Walter's car. He could not say anything that would ease her hurt. He quietly went into his room, picked up his suitcase, and left to catch the bus - the bus that would carry him and several other young men from his neighborhood to the Army camp.

Cousin Nick passed the physical. He was given several days to go home before he was sent to another camp to be trained for service in the war. Before he left, he promised Grandma Jenny faithfully that he would send her money to buy another car.

Cousin Nick was assigned to the Air Force. He was trained to repair the airplanes that flew from one base to another. Sure enough, he sent Grandma Jenny the money to buy another car, but in her heart, it did not fill the place where her beloved Walter left his car. She asked another grandson named I.C. to drive her where she wanted to go.

Every now and then when the family got together, someone would bring up the story of Cousin Nick and Grandma Jenny's car that used to sit in her front yard. They told how Cousin Nick wrecked it; that it had been repaired and running like a new oiled sewing machine; was painted a shiny black and was fitted with a brand new set of white-walled tires.

When the war was over, and Cousin Nick came home he told us exactly what happened on that day. He said, "As I drove along, Jerry played his harmonica and Hubert was singing his favorite song, "Baby, Please Don't Go", when the car went into a dirt bank and turned over. We laughed when we heard this story now, but it was not funny then.

All of our cousins came home from the war. Two of our neighbors' sons were killed in the line of duty. We, in our neighborhood grieved with them.

Thank God! He kept Cousin Nick alive so he could tell his story himself! He is sure glad that God rode with him that particular day!

At that moment, a nurse came into the lounge and interrupted our conversation. "Guess what? The new mother has given birth to twin boys."

"Twins?" said Cousin Wensie. Her eyes were as big as two saucers. "Can we go see the little fellows? I can't wait to see this miracle."

"In a little while," the nurse said. "The doctor is with her at this time. You should be able to see them in the nursery in about a half hour. The nurse left. Immediately Grandma Daisy reached for the walking cane, and began the long walk to the nursery. She peered through the window. There she saw the twins as they lay wrapped snuggly in blankets. Both had gone fast asleep.

Grandma Daisy stared down at the little humans and saw the images of their ancestors reflected in the tiny bodies.

"Our family lives on," she said.

She smiled and went back to the sofa where she sat down because she was tired. Almost immediately, she went to sleep while she told us she was thinking of her family and friends "long gone." This time, the twins were the last family members that Grandma Daisy welcomed into the world.

TALK TO THE TREES
BY
G.R. Anderson
(A story for teaching words)

A.
Tree
Girl
Once upon a time there was a little girl who lived way, way, away in a forest in a far, far, away country.

She had no brothers, nor sisters, not even a dog, cat or bird with which to talk.

So, the little girl "talked" to the trees. Everyday she would walk through the forest and talk to the trees one by one, just as if they were people.

B.
Basket
Parents
Her parents sat and weaved baskets to sell day after day, and they did not talk.

C.
<u>**Animal**</u>
<u>**Tree**</u>
There came a time when her parents became afraid that a large animal would attack her - some animal that they did not know about. So, one morning they told her to choose a special tree to sit under and talk to the tree.

"That way," they said, "we will not worry about you, and you will be close enough to hear us when we call you to dinner."
So, the little girl did as her parents told her. She went into the forest to find a special tree by which to sit.

D.
<u>**Oak Tree**</u>
<u>**Acorn**</u>

First, she sat down by an "**oak**" tree and started to talk to it.

She told the tree of a rabbit that she saw

coming out of a hole. Next, she described a baby turtle that was sleeping in the sun.

Then she told the tree about a caterpillar that was climbing up a tree branch.

The little girl loved to talk, so she spent quite a long time in the forest by the tree.

Sadly, every now and then, an **acorn** would fall on her head.

So she decided that the oak tree would not be a good place to spend the day. She walked away from the oak tree.

E.
Persimmon tree
Persimmons
Birds
The little girl walked a little farther, and saw a "**persimmon**" **tree**.

She sat down and began to talk to it. "Surely this would be the right tree," she thought.

No, the sweet smell of the **persimmons** attracted the **birds** in the area. Sometimes a bird would even land on her head, reaching for the mellow sweet fruit. This tree would definitely not be the one to sit under all day and talk.

F.
Cedar tree
Bugs

Next, she sat down beside a "**cedar**" **tree.** After sitting there for a while, small insects began to fly around her head. The insects, which looked like **bugs,** dropped sticky stuff that fell in her hair.

She decided that the cedar tree would not be a good place to spend the day either.

G.
Pecan tree
She walked on to another tree and sat down. It was a "pecan" tree.

After sitting there for a while, a family of squirrels began to growl at her.

Their home was in the pecan tree. They

wanted her to leave.

"This tree will not do either," she said to herself.

"Anyway, there is too much noise here."

H.
Elm
Tired, the little girl decided to sit under an **"elm" tree.**

While sitting there, nothing pecked at her; and nothing dropped on her.

This was the tree by which she would sit. She sat down and talked, and talked, and talked.

Then she heard her parents' voices calling, "Come to dinner!"

It took only a few minutes for her to arrive for dinner. You see, the elm tree was in her very own backyard.

I.
Kitten
Baskets
One day after the discovery of the elm tree, she got a surprise.

Her father came to the elm tree where she sat, and put a small kitten at her feet. Then he went to work on his baskets.

J.
Kitten
Tree
The **kitten** rubbed the little girl's feet and began to talk to her, using kitten talk.

She finally picked up the kitten and began to talk to it.

At last she had a friend that loved to talk.

No one ever called the little girl's name. As the author, I just called her Little Miss "Talks to the Trees."

The **moral** of the story is that "Sometimes the things we are looking for are closer than we think."

The end.

Legacy of Plays and Drama

"In all thy ways acknowledge Him and He shall direct thy paths." -- Proverbs 3:6

The Road to Calvary

By G.R. Anderson

*Modern-day, copyrighted songs may be used, at the performers' discretion. Licenses for usage must also be obtained at the performers' expense.

Introduction

(Read after the children have entered and are seated.)

Good evening, everyone. When Jesus came into this world, Satan's powers were turned against Jesus.

From the time when Jesus appeared as a babe in Bethlehem, Satan worked to bring about Jesus' destruction. In every possible way, Satan tried to prevent Jesus from developing a perfect childhood, developing a Holy ministry, and from being an unblemished sacrifice.

Satan could not lead Jesus into sin, discourage Him, nor drive Jesus from a work for which He had come on earth to do. From the desert to Calvary, the storm of Satan's wrath beat upon him. But the more it fell, the more the Son of God held on to the hand of His Father.

All efforts of Satan to oppress and overcome Jesus, only brought out a purer and spotless light in Jesus' character. Today our cast will tell the story entitled "The Road to Calvary."

Act 1: "What Is the Charge?"

PROPS: Sanhedrin Court furniture (stage left);
garden (stage right);
space for crosses (center stage)
PERFORMERS:
parent (man or woman), and two (2) children;
4 women mourners
Caiaphas (the high priest)
Pilate and a servant
Nicodemus (wise, leader of the Pharisees)
Two (2) males for Sanhedrin Court counsel
Soldiers (6)
Crowd (various extras)
Simon and two (2) thieves
Soft music plays.
PARENT (Man or Woman) and two children walk through
the city of Jerusalem.
PARENT: (points to the building)
Jerusalem is a beautiful place, full of people who come
here to worship and trade. This is where the Sanhedrin
Court meets.

CHILD 1: What do they do?

PARENT: These men pass judgment on the laws of Moses and try criminal cases.

CHILD 2: Who are the men?

PARENT: They are the elders, the tribal and family heads of the people. They are also priests.

CHILD 1: Do they kill people?

PARENT: No. They can not execute a sentence of death without the permission of the Roman authorities.

CHILD 1: (points to men as they enter from opposite side of stage)
Here they come now.

PARENT: Sh.sh.sh.
Let's sit and listen to them while they hold court.
(Sit in court gallery at corner of stage)

MUSIC PLAYS
MEN: (enter and stand until Caiaphas arrives)

Caiaphas: (enters and sits; soldiers sit)
We will have to silence this man Jesus.

MAN 1: Is that why we are having this meeting?
Caiaphas: Yes. Jesus is disturbing our way of life. We will have to charge him for something to get him out of our way.

MAN 2: What do you have in mind?

Caiaphas: Here is a list of things we could charge him with if we can prove them to be true.

MAN 1: You know the Romans will have to give their approval of what we do.

Caiaphas: (yells) Nicodemus!
NICODEMUS: (enters and stand next to Caiaphas)

Caiaphas: (hands Nicodemus the list)
Nicodemus read this list. Let the council decide what we can charge Jesus with to stop his teaching.

NICODEMUS: But, how sir?

Caiaphas: (stands and walks away angrily)
Find a way.
Find something to charge him with.
I have to attend to the duties for the Temple.

NICODEMUS: (reads from list)
Members of the Council,
The first question on this list says,
"Does Jesus object to paying taxes or
Does He object to Caesar's picture on the coins?"

MAN 1: No.

NICODEMUS: What did He say?
MAN 1: When asked those questions,
He said "Render therefore unto Caesar the things which be Caesar's, and unto God the things which be God's (Luke 20:25 KJV)

NICODEMUS: (reads second question)
Does Jesus violate the Sabbath by working?

MAN 2: Yes, but the people follow Him because he said 'Is it lawful on the Sabbath days to do good, or to do evil? To save life, or to destroy it?' (Luke 6:9)

The scribes and the Pharisees were mad, but they could not do anything.

NICODEMUS: The next question asks, does Jesus teach respect for the temple?

MAN 1: Yes. One day He went to the temple in Jerusalem where He found merchants and money changers.
NICODEMUS: What did He do?

MAN 1: He made a scourge of small cords, drove out the people, the sheep and the oxen; poured out the money, and overthrew the tables. (John 2:14-17 KJV)

MAN 2: He sounds like a man that had gone mad. Maybe we can use that to destroy His teachings.

MAN 1: No. Then He told those who sold doves, '...; make not my Father's house a house of merchandise.' He loves the temple!

NICODEMUS: Okay, does He teach stoning for sinners when they do wrong?

MAN 2: No. He once saw some people getting ready to stone a woman for sinning. Jesus stopped them and said, 'He that is without sin among you, let him first cast a stone at her.' (John 8:7 KJV)
Man, you should have seen them. All of them walked away.

NICODEMUS: What about children? Does He allow children to come hear him preach and teach? You know they make a lot of noise.

MAN 1: That won't work. He said 'Suffer the little children to come unto me, and forbid them not; for of such is the kingdom of God.' (Mark 10:14 KJV)

MAN 2: Then He said, 'Verily I say unto you, whosoever shall not receive the kingdom of God as a little child, he shall not enter therein.'

NICODEMUS: Does He neglect the elderly and the poor?

MAN 1: No! He keeps telling children to 'Honor thy father and thy mother; your days may be long.'

NICODEMUS: I can't find anything which to charge Jesus. Can any of you think of something that He has said or done wrong, so we can use to condemn him?

MAN 2: I think this may be helpful. Jesus must not like rich people for He said that money is the root of all evil. You need money to be rich don't you?

NICODEMUS: (sits as all three rejoice; laughs and throws up coins)
That's it. We'll use the money to trap him!

Audio Visual: Lights dim on the men. Place spotlight on soloist or praise dancers.

SONG: Music continues playing as praise dancers perform

Caiaphas: (enters and confronts the three as they stand for his entrance)
What did you decide?

NICODEMUS: (whispers in Caiaphas' ear)

Caiaphas: (angrily) He did not say that! Jesus said, 'The love of money was the root of all evil.'

MAN 1: That's even better. We will find someone who loves money.

Caiaphas: (sits) I've already found someone. His name is Judas. He is a friend of Jesus' and the treasurer of those rascals.

NICODEMUS: How did you do that?

Caiaphas: I told him I wanted to meet Jesus. I explained that when Jesus is speaking there are always too many people around him for me to talk privately. I asked when could I see him and where does he go when he rests for the night?

MAN 2: Did you entrap him with that?

Caiaphas: Not at first. Then I told him that I would make it worth his troubles. (tosses three (3) coins on the floor)
Right away Judas told me that they go to a garden. He said that Jesus rests and prays.
NICODEMUS: Where is this garden?

Caiaphas: Judas is going to show me.

MAN 1: But it is going to be dark. How will we know who to arrest?

Caiaphas: Judas assured me that the man he greets with a kiss will be him.

NICODEMUS: I just don't believe that. How much did you give him to betray his friend?

Caiaphas: (smiles; points to the coins on the floor)
Thirty (30) pieces of silver.
You three must depart now, but we will meet with Judas and his group tomorrow night. Send the soldiers in so I may tell them what they must do.

NICODEMUS, MAN 1 AND MAN 2: (exit)

SOLDIERS: (enter with swords and spears)

Caiaphas: You men come with me. I have heard that Nicodemus went to visit Jesus one night. He may be on Jesus' side. So we will go to the garden tonight. We will arrest Jesus and take Him with us to be questioned. I don't want his followers warned and see us coming for Jesus.

Caiaphas and SOLDIERS: (exit stage in opposite direction of the first three)

Song: "I Know It Was the Blood" or
"I've Decided to Make Jesus My Choice"

ACT 2: The Road to Calvary
Scene 1: Garden of Gethsemane (stage right)

Jesus and eleven (11) Disciples enter.
Jesus kneels to pray.
Disciples sit and sleep.

Jesus: (stops praying and looks at His Disciples sleeping)
Wake up. Wake up.
Can you not tarry with me for a little while?

Disciples: (arise and points to someone coming)

Judas: (walks on stage toward Jesus; then kisses Him)

Soldier: (grabs Jesus' arm)

Peter: (raises sword and strikes the soldier. Soldier removes ear replica).

Jesus: No Peter. Those who live by the sword shall die by the sword.
(Jesus takes ear and places it back on the soldier)

Think thou that I can not now pray to my Father and he shall presently give me more than twelve legions of Angels? Take me as it is written.

All: (exit)

Nicodemus: (looking worried enters the garden; stage right) I have learned that Jesus was arrested after we left the meeting last night.
He was carried to the house of Ananias, the High Priest.
He was tried there.
They charged Him with blasphemy!
They said he put himself equal to God.
But He never said He was equal to God.
I will go see for myself. (exits)

Pilate: (sits in courtyard; stage right)

Soldier: (brings Jesus to Pilate)
All honor to Pilate.
Caiaphas, the high Priest of the Sanhedrin court has sent this Jesus to be judged in your court.

Pilate: (angrily)
Why did you bring him here?
What accusations did those Jews bring against Him?
If He is not a criminal, why bring Him to me?
I have spoken to this man before.
I can find no fault in Him. My wife even had bad dreams about this man and said that I should have nothing to do with Him.
Servant, bring me some water in a bowl.
I wash my hands of this matter.

Servant: (enters carrying bowl and a towel; approaches Pilate.)
Pilate: (washes hands and points to servant to exit.)

Soldier: But, sir. The custom is that when the Jews have a feast, one prisoner must be released.

Pilate: And whom did they choose?

Soldier: Don't you hear them?
They chose Barabbas, who was to be put to death.
They said, to crucify this Christ.
Pilate: Then so be it.

Soldier: (forces Jesus off stage)
Pilate: (loudly)

But take Him and let His own people deal with him. (exits)
Lights dim.

Scene 2: CALVARY

Song: *Soloist sings "Calvary"*

3 Soldiers: (enter while soloist sings. Bring in 3 crosses.
Places one cross on floor at stage entrance;
Stands one cross on left stage.
Stands one cross on right stage)
Crowd and 2 Soldiers *(enter with 2 thieves.*
Ties one to cross on left and one to cross on right)

Soldier: *(enters with Jesus. Stops at stage entrance. Points to cross on floor.)*
Here is your cross.
You will have to carry it up the hill by yourself.

Jesus: Stumbles as He tries to pick up the cross.

Soldier: (turns to crowd)
You, Simon!

Come help this man carry this cross.

Simon: Takes cross and helps Jesus carry it.

4 Women (enter weeping and singing as Jesus and Simon are led to center stage)
Song: "Were You There When They Crucified My Lord?"

Soldier: (Strips Jesus of His robe as others tie Him to the cross.)

Jesus: (raises head) I thirst.

Soldier: (holds up stick and Ragon soaked in vinegar)

Jesus: *(turns head away; looks at weeping women)*
Daughters of Jerusalem.
Weep not for me.
But weep for yourselves.

Soldier: If thou be the king of the Jews, save thou self! (laughs; places crown of thorns on Jesus' head.)

Thief 1: If you be Christ, save yourself and us.

Thief 2: We are receiving our just reward for our deeds
But this man has done nothing wrong.
(Turns to Jesus)
Jesus, Lord remember me when thou come into thy kingdom.

Jesus: Verily I say unto thee, today shalt thou be with me in Paradise. Father forgive them for they know not what they do.

Audio Visual (lights flash to represent the image of lightning; drums beat; thunder roars)

Soldier: (Covers eyes. Screams)
Truly this was the Son of God!
Jesus: My God
My God
Why has thou forsaken me?
Father into thy hands I commit my Spirit. It is finished.

Audio Visual: *Lights dim. Thunder roars.*
Lightening flashes.

Song: *Music plays.*

Joseph: *(Takes Jesus from the cross)*

People: *exit*

Soldiers: *Carries two (2) thieves from the cross.*

Audio visual: Lights brighten.

Praise Dancers: (perform)

Jesus: *(re-enters, dressed in white robe; looks at empty crosses)* O grave where is thy victory? O death where is thy sting?

Jesus: *(turns to audience)*
Bless is he who believes and not seen. Go ye therefore and teach all nations, baptizing them in the name of the Father and of the Son and of the Holy Ghost; teaching them to observe all things whatsoever I commanded you. And lo, I am with you always even to the end of the world.

Song: entire cast enters singing *"Halleluiah Chorus"*

Fruits of the Spirit

By G. R. Anderson

Modern-day, copyrighted songs may be used, at the performers discretion. Licenses for usage must also be obtained at the performers' expense.

The Program
Opening Song
Prayer
Welcome Psalms 15:1-2
Song
Narrator Introduction
Song (Cast marches in)
1ˢᵗ Speaker LOVE
2ⁿᵈ Speaker JOY
3ʳᵈ Speaker PEACE
4ᵗʰ Speaker LONG SUFFERING
5ᵗʰ Speaker GENTLENESS
6ᵗʰ Speaker GOODNESS
7ᵗʰ Speaker FAITH
8ᵗʰ Speaker MEEKNESS
9ᵗʰ Speaker TEMPERANCE
Conclusion

Speaker 1:
Reads scripture - Psalms 15:1-2

Lord, who shall abide in thy tabernacle
And who shall dwell in they Holy hill?
He that walketh uprightly and worketh righteousness and speaketh the truth in his heart.

(Looks at audience)
Welcome   to   today's   production   by   the
_____ Drama Ministry.

Our play is entitled "The Fruits of the Spirit" as written by

Mrs. Gertrude R. Anderson with scripture references from the Apostle Paul in Galatians 5:22.

We welcome you, and hope you are inspired by our cast of performers.

Our praise dancers will now do battle with the "evil spirit" that is always present and looking for whom he can kill, steal, and destroy.

Let's welcome our praise dancers as they battle the spirit they call the strong man of evil.

NARRATOR:

Paul, an Apostle of Jesus Christ - and God the Father - wrote to the brethren in the churches in Galatia and said "Brethren, the Gospel I preach is not after man. It is by the revelation of Jesus Christ."

Man is not justified by the works of the law, but by faith in Jesus Christ. He put His spirit in us. When we walk in the spirit of Jesus, we will bear fruit.

Those fruits are LOVE,
JOY,
PEACE,
LONGSUFFERING,
GENTLENESS,
GOODNESS,
FAITH,
MEEKNESS,
AND TEMPERANCE.

CAST: (enters singing "Fruits of the Spirit" arranged by Mrs. G. Anderson)

Fruits of the Spirit
(Sung to Melody of "Give Me That Old Time Religion")

Chorus:
By their fruits you shall know them.
By their fruits you shall know them.

Let the fruits of the Spirit
Dwell in your hearts today.
Verse 1:
There is Love in the Spirit
Verse 2:
There is Joy in the Spirit.
Verse 3:
There is Goodness in the Spirit.
Chorus:
By their fruits you shall know them.
By their fruits you shall know them.
Let the fruits of the Spirit
Dwell in your hearts today.

Each speaker enters wearing a "fruit" sign.
1st Speaker: I bring you the first fruit of the Spirit.
It is LOVE. It means being close to another - by affection of FAITH. Love worketh no ill or wrong doing to his neighbor. Therefore, love is the fulfillment of the law. John 3:16 says, "For God so loved the world that He gave His only begotten son, that whosoever believeth in Him shall not perish, but have everlasting life.

Sounds: *Drum music plays.*

2nd Speaker: The second fruit of the spirit is JOY. Joy is when you know the Lord has blessed your family and neighbors. Joy is when the Lord has healed you or someone you love. Joy is a condition of supreme well-being. "Restore unto me the JOY of my strength, and uphold me with thy free Spirit," David asked the Lord after David had sinned. "The JOY of the Lord is my strength," he continued. They that sow in tears shall reap in joy.

Song: (a non-copyrighted song)
Sounds: *Drum music plays.*

3rd Speaker : The third fruit of the spirit is PEACE. Be not quarrelsome, unruly or name calling. Remember that a soft voice turns away wrath. The fruit of righteousness is sown in the peace of them that make peace. Jesus said before He left, "My peace I leave with you."

4th Speaker: The fourth fruit of the spirit is LONGSUFFERING. That means enduring hardship or inconvenience without complaining. Bear ye one another's burdens. Think of the woman that suffered 12 long years with an issue of blood. She simply touched the hem of Jesus' garment. Jesus felt her longsuffering and prayers, and healed her. She waited on Jesus and believed in His mercy.

Song: (a non-copyrighted song)
Sounds: *Drum music plays.*

5th Speaker: The fifth fruit of the Spirit is GENTLENESS. Being free from violence within and without is the key. The servant of the Lord must not be mean, but be gentle unto all people. It is similar to being gentle with a baby brother or sister, and helping them to learn to eat by themselves, or helping them to learn to walk. Remember Jesus when He was talking to the children and the grown-ups. He said, "Suffer little children to come unto me for such is the kingdom of heaven.

Sounds: *Drum music plays.*
6th Speaker: The sixth fruit of the spirit is GOODNESS which is having pleasant and desirable ways. Be kind and concerned for others. Instead of saying bad things about one's brother or sister, say or do something that will lift them. Think of something good about the person. If you can't say something good, don't say anything. You didn't walk in their shoes, so you are not qualified to judge.

Sounds: *Drum music plays.*

7th Speaker: The seventh fruit of the spirit is FAITH. Faith is the substance of things hoped for; the evidence of things not seen. It is also the mental acceptance of the truth of something. You are the children of God, by faith in Jesus Christ. Jesus said that if you have the faith of a mustard seed, you can say unto the mountain, remove thee from your place, and it should move.

Sounds: *Drum music plays.*

8th Speaker: The eighth fruit of the spirit is MEEKNESS. Matthew 5:5 says "Blessed are the meek, for they shall inherit the earth. Be not deceived. God is not mocked. Whatever a man soweth, that shall he reap. Jesus said, Take my yoke upon you and learn of me, for I am meek and lowly in heart, and ye shall find rest for your soul, for my yoke is easy and my burden is light.

Song: (children sing)

Sound: *Drum music plays.*

9th Speaker: The ninth fruit of the spirit is TEMPERANCE. That means avoiding extreme loudness in matters of conversation. Control your feelings and temper in personal conduct with others. Jesus said, You have not chosen me, but I have chosen you, and ordained you, that you should go and bring forth fruit, and that your fruit should remain, that whatsoever ye should ask of the Father, in my name, He may give it to you. These things I command you, that you love one another. I have something to tell those who have been on this Christian journey, and walking in the Fruits of the Spirit, for a long time.

Song: (a non copyrighted song)

Sound: *Drum music plays.*

10th Speaker: When we walk in the spirit of Jesus, we will

bear fruit. Those fruits are
LOVE,
JOY,
PEACE,
LONGSUFFERING,
GENTLENESS,
GOODNESS,
FAITH,
MEEKNESS, AND
TEMPERANCE.

Sound: *Drum music plays.*

Our Redeemer:
Jesus, the Promise

By Gertrude R. Anderson

Adapted from the books of Luke and Matthew from the King James Version of the Bible.

*Modern-day, copyrighted songs may be used, at the performer's discretion. Licenses for usage must also be obtained at the performers' expense.

Actors must dress according to the characters they play to inspire viewers.

The scene opens with a teacher and her students sitting in a half-circle.

Teacher - *Good morning, young people!*
Today we are going to talk about why we celebrate Christmas.
But first we will listen to some of the things that happened many years ago before the Christmas celebrations began.
We have learned from our Bible study that God appointed Angels to watch over people.
While we are sitting here, we will close our eyes and listen to the Angels in our Christmas play, tell the story.

(Students sit down, close their eyes and listen as the Angels enter).

1ˢᵗ Angel -
I am Gabriel, a messenger of God.
I was sent by God to tell a young virgin named Mary that she would bring forth a son. His name shall be called "Jesus". He shall save his people from their sins. I also appeared to Joseph and told him to take Mary for his wife and that her son was to be of the Holy Ghost.

75

(Go to side of the stage and sit in chairs.)

Three angels and three shepherds enter together.

2nd *Angel* -
We appeared to the shepherds while they were tending their sheep in the fields.
I said to them, "Fear not - I bring you tidings of great joy - For unto you is born this day in the city of David - A Savior- which is Christ the Lord. You shall find him wrapped in swaddling clothes - lying in a manger.
A multitude of Heavenly host sang "Glory to God in the highest and on earth - peace- goodwill to toward men.

Exit. Sit in chairs.

Song --- Silent Night

3rd *Angel* -
That night the baby Jesus was born.
Wise men had seen the Christ child's star - and followed it. When they came upon Herod - the King - they told him that a special child was being born - and they were going to give him gifts.
Hearing this Herod told them when they find the baby - come back and tell him where the baby could be found.
But God appeared to the shepherds in a dream and told them to go home another way - Herod was seeking the child to kill him.

Exit. Sit in chairs.

Angel enters with Simeon, a just man with a beard

4th *Angel* -
The Holy Spirit revealed to a just man named Simeon that he would not see death before he had seen the Lord's Christ.

When he had seen the Christ child - he said,
"Mine eyes have seen thy Salvation - now let thy servant depart in peace."
We Angels remained with the Holy Family - and watched over them - day and night.

Exit. Sit in chairs.

Song *- "Angels We Have Heard On High"*

Angel enters.

5th Angel -
Meanwhile - King Herod continued to search for the baby Jesus. The King thought the baby would take his place as King.

Exit. Sit in chairs.

Angel enters

6th Angel -
King Herod had his soldiers kill all the baby boys under the age of two years. He hoped one of them would be the Christ Child.
Matthew 2:18 says, "There was great weeping - Rachel weeping for her children - and would not be comforted."
For a long time we listened to the moans - and groans of many mothers in the land - as they cried out to God.

Rachel enters weeping, then exit.

Angel enters.

7th Angel -
The heavenly Father sent me to Joseph - the husband of Mary. - in a dream and told me to say to him "Arise - take the young child and his mother - and flee to Egypt. Herod

is seeking the child - to kill him.

Angel leads the Holy family offstage.

8th Angel -

We Angels guided the Holy family to Egypt - and stayed with them. After Herod died - The Lord of heaven said "Out of Egypt - Have I called my Son."

Exit. Sit in chairs.

Angel enters.

9th Angel -

The Holy Family returned and settled in Galilee of Nazareth. Our Angel job guarding the Baby Jesus from Herod was completed. The Baby Jesus grew up to be a man - and was the Savior of the world.

Exit.

Jesus (male adult) comes to the front of the stage and blesses people. Jesus exits.

Teacher -

Open your eyes!
Now do you understand why we celebrate Christmas?
It is the Baby Jesus' birthday. He is God's gift to mankind.
But this is just the beginning of His life being told.

All sing closing song - "*Go Tell It On The Mountain*"
All exit as they sing.

The Thirteenth Disciple:

Testimonies of the Disciples
By Mrs. Gertrude Richmond Anderson

Adapted from Acts 1:23, 24, 25

*Modern-day, copyrighted songs may be used, at the performer's discretion. Licenses for usage must also be obtained at the performers' expense.

Narrator and Cast:
1. Simon Peter
2. Andrew
3. James (the son of Zebedee)
4. John (the brother of James)
5. Phillip
6. Bartholomew
7. Thomas
8. Matthew (the publican, son of Alpheus)
9. James (son of Alpheus)
10. Thaddeus
11. Simon the Canaanite
12. Judas Iscariot
13. Matthias

The Thirteenth Disciple:
Testimonies of the Disciples

SCENE: The 11 disciples sit at a table. Matthias and three (3) others sit apart from them.
Judas Iscariot's chair sits empty.

Narrator:
Our Lord Jesus was betrayed by Judas Iscariot, the 12th disciple listed in the book of Matthews. He betrayed Jesus with a kiss and for thirty pieces of silver.

Jesus was crucified, bled and died on Golgotha Hill which is to say, a place of skulls. Jesus was buried in Joseph's new tomb.

On the third day He rose, as he said he would. He then appeared several times to his disciples; after which He ascended unto heaven to be with His Father.

Some time later, the eleven disciples met to select another disciple to replace Judas. After much prayer, they cast lots between Joseph, Barsebos Justus, and Matthias. The lot fell upon Matthias, and he was added to the eleven disciples.

In this scene, disciples are welcoming him to the group by introducing themselves and telling him some of the experiences they had with Jesus. Peter stands to prepare to conduct the meeting.
(Exits)

Peter: *(standing)*
Brethren, we have a new member with us today. (points) Brother Matthias. Let us welcome him. *(hand claps)*

Matthias: *(stand; then sits down)*

Peter:
Brother Matthias, I am Simon Peter, Jesus' first disciple. So I will speak first. I was a fisherman fishing in the seas of Galilee when Jesus came by one day and said to me "Come and I will make you fishers of men". From that day on I followed Him.

One day He asked me "Who do men say I am"?
I answered, "Thou are the Christ, the son of the living God."

Jesus said, "Thou art Peter, and upon this rock I will build my church."

When Jesus' enemies came for Him, I denied Him three times saying, "I didn't know Him."

Later, I wept bitter tears for denying Him, but Jesus knew that my spirit was willing but the flesh was weak, and He forgave me.

I was an unstable and outspoken man, but Jesus molded me into a man of stability, and gave me the courage to be a faithful follower in the word.

As a result, I became the spokesman for the disciples who would come later.
(sits.)

Andrew: *(stands)*
I'm Andrew, the second disciple called. I'm the brother of Simon Peter and the son of Jonas of Galilee was also a fisherman.
John the Baptist directed me to Jesus, and said Jesus was the "Lamb of God". I was with Jesus when He performed many miracles, especially when He fed the thousand people with five loaves of bread and two fish. *(sits)*

James: *(stands)*
I am James, the third disciple, the son of Zebedee, and the older brother of John. We were called the Sons of Thunder. I was with Jesus when he raised Jairus' daughter.
I was also with Him at the transfiguration. I was with Him during the agony in the garden of Gethsemane before His crucifixion. *(sits down)*

John: *(stands)*
I am John, the fourth disciple. I am also the brother of James and one of the Sons of Thunder. It was said that we always talked loudly and long. So this name was given to us. I was with our Lord Jesus until the end. *(sits down)*

Phillip: *(stands)*
I am Phillip, the fifth disciple. In the beginning, I was a disciple of John the Baptist, until he pointed me to Jesus. I do not talk much, but I introduced Nathaniel to Jesus. I was among the disciples in the upper chamber before Pentecost. *(sits down)*

Bartholomew: (stands)
I am Bartholomew, the sixth disciple listed among the disciples. I was a faithful follower of Jesus, and I still am. *(sits down)*

Thomas: *(stands)*
My name is Thomas, the seventh disciple, called Didymus. I was slow to believe. At first, I did not believe in the resurrection. When Jesus appeared after His crucifixion and showed me the nail scars in His hands, and the wound in His side, he told me to feel them for myself. When I did, I immediately said to Him, "My Lord, and my God".
Jesus said, "Blessed is he that have not seen but believe." I saw Jesus again when He appeared on the Sea of Galilee and in the Upper Room in Jerusalem. I'm a witness that He rose. *(sits down)*

Matthew: *(stands)*
I am Matthew, the eighth disciple, the son of Alpheus and I am a Publican. I am also called Levi. I was a tax collector at Capernaum when Jesus called me. I am skilled in writing and in keeping records. I am thankful for that, because I also recorded Jesus' miracles and life. *(sits down)*

James: (stands)
I am James the ninth disciple and also the son of Alpheus. I am a witness for Jesus also. (sits down)

Thaddeus: (stands)
I am Thaddeus, the tenth disciple. I was a faithful follower of Jesus and I will be a witness for Him. (sits)

Simon: (stands)
I am Simon the eleventh disciple and a Canaanite. I was called a Zealot which means I was and still am very serious abut my devotion to Jesus. *(sits down)*

Peter: *(stands again and points to Judas' chair)*
This chair was once occupied by Judas Iscariot, the 12th disciple. He was our treasurer. He had hoped to have a high place in Jesus' Kingdom here on earth. He did not understand and care about the message of love and God's Kingdom. Satan entered his heart and he betrayed our Lord Jesus with a kiss. Judas accepted payment for the betrayal, and for thirty pieces of silver, Jesus was put to death. When Judas realized the awful thing that he had done, he went out and hanged himself. That poor soul!
(Moves Judas' chair. Places another in its stead.)
We must not leave the work undone. We have cast votes to fill a void. We selected someone of noble character, and is devout.
After continued prayer, and God's answer, the lot goes to Matthias.
Brother Matthias, come and be seated with us. You are our 13th chosen disciple.

Before Jesus left us, He taught us many things. Brother Matthias, we will teach you what you need to know.

Jesus gave us a prayer to pray; a commandment to keep, and a job to do. *(Begins to pray as the others join in)*

Our Father, which art in Heaven,
Hallowed be thy name.
Thy kingdom come.
Thy will be done in earth,
as it is in heaven.
Give us this day our daily bread,
and forgive us our debts
as we forgive our debtors.
And lead us not into temptation,
but deliver us from evil.
For thine is the kingdom,
and the power,
and the glory,
forever,
Amen.

James*: (stands)*
The first Commandment was that thou shalt love the Lord thy God with all thy heart, and with all thy soul, and with all thy mind. This is the first as well as the greatest commandment.

The second was like unto it that thou thy shall love thy neighbor as thyself.

John: *(stands)*
The job is to do as Jesus did, "Go ye therefore, and teach all nations, baptizing them in the name of the father, and of the Son, and of the Holy Ghost/ Teaching them to observe all things. Whatsoever I have commanded you, and lo I am with you always, even unto the end of the world.

Peter: (still standing)
Our Lord Jesus also said, "Remember me…" He told us to do this in remembrance of Him.

(Picks up bread and passes to all of the disciples, then hold His bread up so all can see it.)

Take, eat, this is my body..
(eats the bread then pours wine in the cups; and passes cups to all of the disciples)
Drink ye all of it; for this is my blood of the new testament which is shed for many for the remission of sins. Do this in remembrance of him.

(All drink the wine; begin singing Amazing Grace).

(Exit stage)

Changed Mah (My) Name
By G.R. Anderson

Black History

*Modern-day, copyrighted songs may be used, at the performer's discretion. Licenses for usage must also be obtained at the performers' expense.

Characters march in from both sides of stage singing "Plenty Good Room In My Father's Kingdom…There's Room For Many 'A More"

Introduction (read aloud by narrator)
(choir sings Kum Bah Yah, softly.)
Welcome to another Black History Program.

Today, we would like to present to you a play entitled "Changed Mah Name". It is a play about slavery, and the redemption for the Black people in America. As far back as anyone can remember, slavery has been practiced by many cultures and in many countries, even during Bible times.

We will focus our attention on the continent of Africa, the home of our ancestors and their dilemma. In Africa, when the chiefs made war with neighboring tribes and won the battle, they took prisoners and made them slaves within the tribe. Sometimes they married into the tribe.

When the village became crowded with these people, many of them were sold to anyone who wanted to buy them. Sometimes they even stole people from other villages and sold them also.

There are greedy and cruel people in all cultures. During that time, the Arabs bought many of the Black people but the Europeans were responsible for the bulk of the slave trade. They brought their slaves to this country and sold them to the highest bidder.

A few free Blacks came with them freely but the majority of them came on the slave ships against their will. Our story begins with a conversation with one of the people who had just gotten off the ship, and came in contact with the slave merchants here in America.

Song: Kum Bah Yah

ACT 1: AFRICAN DRESS
One Man's Story

Speaker: *(Points to others)*
The slave catchers stole us from our homes in Africa and now sold us to the plantation owners here. The first thing they did was changed my name!

My name is Mbois. They changed it to Toby.
His name is Cosmo Koko. They changed it to Catman.
Her name is Ajaka. They changed it to Violet.
Her name is Okeke. They changed it to Petunia.
How dare they!
These slave owners are destroying our language. We are not allowed to speak it anymore.
They are destroying our families by selling us one by one. We don't know where our family members are, but the one thing I will never forget is how they changed by name and tried to make me forget who I was.
I know my name! And I know who I am! (EXIT)

Sounds: *drum beats and the shaking of rattlers*

ACT II: A STRANGE LAND - SLAVE DRESS

SCENE 1
Song: "I Couldn't Hear Nobody Pray"

(A woman enters; holds up a Bible, then the book of Little Black Sambo.)

Speaker: Look at this. The slave owners used the Holy Bible to make us satisfied to be a slave. They let us go to their church and listen to their preacher. They read this scripture almost every time we went there.

(Reads scripture - "Servant obey your Master...")
Then they said "You were to be servants for us."
Then they said we were cursed because of our color. For a long time we were ashamed of our ancestors.
Next they read a book called Little Black Sambo that showed Black children ignorant and ugly. This so-called children's story made Blacks hate themselves because they were black and they were called nigger.
(Hold up picture.)
They were not told to be proud of who they were, and to see beauty in being black. *(Exit)*

Song: "I Know I've Been Changed"

Narrator: The slave families had to attend to their own health needs. They learned to use the roots and herbs around them to cure their sickness. When a slave died that person was carried to what they called the "bone yard".
Sometimes their friends walked the last mile to the graveyard with them, but usually only those who carried the burial box was allowed to leave the fields. Many times their friends had already had their "sit up with dying" service.
Listen to one woman comforting her dying friend.

SCENE 2

(Group of women and children enter dressed in mourning clothing, preferably sack cloths.)

Woman: *(Reads poem, "Go Down Death" by James Weldon Johnson. Exit.)*

Song: "I Got Shoes. You Got Shoes"

SCENE 3

Man: *(Enters. Talks to women.)*
It's selling time!
(Puts a "For Sale" sign around the child's neck. Child waves to Mother and cries as being led away by man. Women exit.)

Narrator: Through toil, sweat and tears, the Black people tamed a wilderness and called it America. Their work day began at daybreak and ended at sundown.
There were blacksmiths, carpenters, people who worked in the houses and with cattle.

The majority worked in the fields. Many plantation owners hired men called "overseers" who used whips to make the people work faster. These were usually cruel men. If there were slow workers who could not work any faster, this caused trouble. They were traded or sold on the auction block to the highest bidder.

Listen as one woman experiences the heart-wrenching separation from her child.

Song: *"Good bye.. If I never see you no more…Pray for me… Fare thee well."*

SCENE 4

(Black child enters following white child. White child sits to read. Black child looks over white child's shoulder. White child passes book to Black child who now smiles and reads. Exit.)

(White preacher enters with Bible, preaching and praising God. Black man follows. White man stops. Turns. Hands book to Black man. Exit. Black man begins to reading and preaching. Exit.)

Narrator: The slave owners passed laws that kept Black people in submission. One law stated that it was against the law to teach a Black person to read. However, you know how we are - tell us not to do something - or attach our intelligence by saying we don't have the brains to do it and we will find a way to prove the theory wrong.
The children learned to read by watching the owners' children learn to read. The black preachers learned the scriptures by listening to the plantation preachers when they were allowed to attend services at their church in a corner reserved for Blacks. They loved to hear them preach about Moses and how he delivered the children of Israel from bondage.
Slaves wore ragged clothing that was many times dirty. Yet it made them immune to many of the diseases that the slave owners died off. The Blacks trusted in God and had Christian brothers and sisters to help them keep the faith, and prayed that one day they all would be free.

Slave: *(Enters and read the poem "When Ol' Sister Judy Prayed")*

Song: **"Hold On. Hold On."** *Ask audience to hold hands together.*

SCENE 5

Narrator: These actions caused a conflict between the States of the North and those of the South. The United States became a Nation Divided.

Without the labor of the people in slavery, the people of the South could not continue to live in the style they were enjoying.

However, not all in the South like the system of slavery. Some secretly worked to rid the country of the evil institution called Slavery.

The Northern States depended on the materials from the South to operate their factories. No compromise was reached that included the freeing of the slaves.

Then a Civil War began and the Black people were caught in the middle. Black men became run-a-ways and joined the Northern Army. Some of them that were still on the Southern Plantation were sent to aid the Southern soldiers many times as body servants to their owners.

When the battles were over, many soldiers lay dead on both sides, and the Black people were set free.

Yet other problems awaited them. The main problem was how to live in a free society. They had always been told what to do and what not to do.

Song: "Free At Last... Thank God almighty, I'm Free At Last" *(Performers clap hands and jump up and down.)*

Woman: *(Recites poem "Mother To Son" by Langston Hughes, available on the internet. After reading, woman says):* "You must pass songs to the next generation. *(Exit)*

Narrator: Freedom has a price. Black people soon began

to pay for freedom with many challenges. Booker T. Washington got the schools he wanted and began the education process. His method was necessary.

His motto was "Let down your bucket where you are" which meant prepare yourself and make things better where you are before you go to work trying to change the laws and entering politics.

One famous institution that Washington made famous was Tuskegee. It proved to be more important during World War II when Black men were trained to fly airplanes on their property.

W.E.B. Dubois got his wish also. It came many years later. Black people would once again raise their hearts and hands to God for directions.

Song: "We've Come This Far By Faith"

SCENE 6 A New Day … A New Dream

Two Men: (Enter dressed to look like Martin Luther King and Thurgood Marshall, a lawyer. Carry torches.)

King: I am Dr. Martin Luther King. With me is Thurgood Marshall.

Marshall: I am a talented Black lawyer.

King: I was a minister and carried the Torch of Freedom for my people when their freedom was abused. I gave hope and encouragement. I was a winner of the National Nobel Peace Prize for my work of peace and equal rights for all people.

Marshall: Dr. King, please recite some parts of your "I Have A Dream" speech. It might live in the hearts of Black people for many years to come.

King: We want first class citizenship. You can do it now. I may not get to the Promised Land, but I have been to the mountain top.

Marshall: We have always believed that we were entitled to full citizenship - by right of birth - by right of toil - by right of defense of our country. *(Exit.)*

Narrator: *(Takes torches.)*
Today we hand the torch of Freedom to the next generation. Will our college students come forward please? *(Gives one candle to the first student to be passed down to the last student.)*
You must pass it to the next generation.

Song: "We've Come A Long Way"

Narrator: We have come a long way, praising God. Give Him a hand clap of praise for He Is good and He is merciful. There was a time in the past when our ancestors' names were changed against their will.
When other people have the power to change your name, they have complete power.
Today as Christians, our names have been changed by choice - from sinners to saints of God - working for His glory.

Soloist: Jesus said in John 15:7 - "If you abide in me, and my words abide in you - You shall ask what you will - and it shall be done unto you. Come on lets praise His name!

Song: *I told Jesus it would be alright if He changed my name. I told Jesus I would give Him the glory, if He changed my name. I'm so glad - I'm so glad - Jesus changed my name.*

(*Modern-day, copyrighted songs may be used, at the performers' discretion. Licenses for usage must also be obtained at the performers' expense.)

Gertrude Richmond Anderson